Henry e. Niles

Commemoration of Twenty-five Years of Service

by the Rev. Henry E Niles, D.D., as Pastor of the First Presbyterian Church

1865-1890

Henry e. Niles

Commemoration of Twenty-five Years of Service
*by the Rev. Henry E Niles, D.D., as Pastor of the First Presbyterian Church
1865-1890*

ISBN/EAN: 9783337816094

Printed in Europe, USA, Canada, Australia, Japan

Cover: Foto ©Lupo / pixelio.de

More available books at **www.hansebooks.com**

1865.  1890.

COMMEMORATION

OF

TWENTY-FIVE YEARS OF SERVICE

BY THE

REV. HENRY E. NILES, D.D.,

AS PASTOR OF

THE FIRST

PRESBYTERIAN CHURCH,

YORK, PA.

ALSO A SKETCH

OF THE

EARLY HISTORY OF THE CHURCH.

1865   Ebenezer   1890

Shiloh   Salem

Bethel   Genesis

1860   Alleluia   1762

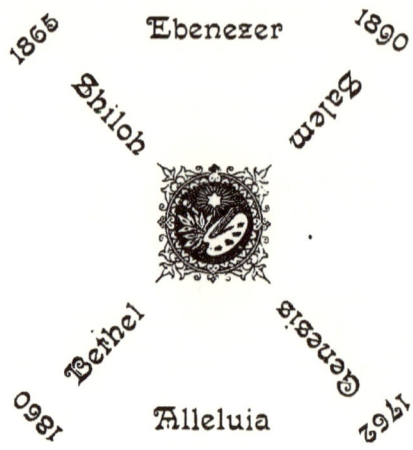

YORK, PA.,
HUBLEY PRINTING CO., L'D,
1890.

*"We have thought of Thy loving kindness,
O God, in the midst of Thy temple."*

CONTENTS.

PREFATORY.

IN view of the fact that the twenty-fifth anniversary of the settlement of our pastor would soon arrive, a conference of members of the congregation was called at the close of the Wednesday evening service, March 12, 1890. A proposition for the public observance of that event being unanimously approved, the following were chosen an executive committee to devise measures for the suitable execution of that plan, viz:

MRS. DAVID E. SMALL,
MR. JOHN M. BROWN,
MR. JOHN H. SMALL.

At subsequent meetings this committee made various reports, and at length the following sub-committees were appointed:

Committee on Invitations.

HENRY SMALL, *Chairman.*

JOSEPH ROOT,	JAMES KELL, ESQ.,
DR. M. J. McKINNON,	MISS ANNA M. SMALL,
MRS. JOHN H. SMALL,	MRS. A. R. BLAIR,

MISS M. E. PRINCE.

Committee on Decorations.

GEORGE S. BILLMEYER, *Chairman.*

WM. H. SOUDER,	MRS. G. E. HERSH,
GUY H. BOYD,	MRS. H. M. CRIDER,
WM. A. COOK,	MRS. GEO. S. BILLMEYER,
MISS FANNIE M. UPP,	MISS LUCY A. CASE,

MISS FANNIE E. EVANS.

Committee on Programme.

H. C. NILES, ESQ. *Chairman.*

DR. B. F. SPANGLER,	MRS. H. W. McCALL,
JAMES McLEAN,	MRS. C. J. WELSH,
DR. J. F. SMALL,	MISS E. MENOUGH.

Committee on Music.

WM. H. HERMAN, *Chairman.*

C. H. THOMAS,	MRS. A. A. LONG,
JOHN A. JONES,	MISS MAZIE FISHER,
MISS BESSIE M. DAVIS,	MISS CARRIE KEYSER,

MISS M. LOUISE WEISER.

Committee on Entertainment.

Wm. H. McClellan, *Chairman.*

Dr. Henry Ness, Miss Louisa Durkee,
Dr. A. A. Long, Miss Mary E. Kell,
Charles M. Billmeyer, Miss C. E. Adams,
Harry D. Rupp, Miss Annie V. Rupp,
Edward P. Stair, Mrs. David Strickler,
Mrs. C. B. Wallace, Mrs. Clara Strawinski,
Mrs. Samuel Small, Mrs. J. A. Weiser,
David E. Small, Mrs. Jno. M. Brown,
Henry R. Kraber, Mrs. II. A. Ebert,
Mrs. Edward Chapin.

Committee on Finance.

Charles I. Nes, *Chairman.*

Isaac A. Elliott, Wm. H. Griffith,
Wm. F. Ramsay, James A. Kell,
John Hamilton Small,
J. Bailey Sayres.

Subsequently, the following card of invitation was issued by the committee to be addressed to every family connected with the Church, and to former members in and out of the city :

1865

You are invited to attend
the services in celebration of

The Twenty-Fifth Anniversary

of the installation of

Rev. Henry E. Niles, D. D.

as pastor of the

First Presbyterian Church,
of York, Pa.,

Sunday, April 6th, 1890.

1890

ANNIVERSARY EXERCISES.

IT was Easter Sabbath, and the weather proved excep-
tionally spring-like and beautiful. The decorations
of the church were elaborate and eminently appropriate. From the centre of the ceiling hung festoons
of evergreen running to each of the corners and ter-
minating in graceful pendants. Over each of the windows
was one of the words, "Diligence," "Faith," "Virtue,"
"Knowledge," "Temperance," "Patience," "Godliness,"
"Brotherly Kindness," "Charity." The pillars on either
side of the pulpit recess were covered with smilax and
calla lilies, and their bases set in beds of palms and ferns,
while in front of the desk was a bank of Easter lilies in
their splendor of green and whiteness. Over the pulpit
was suspended in large letters, the word "Ebenezer."
Over the choir gallery the word "Alleluia." Around each
of the circular end windows were these symbolic inscrip-
tions: "Genesis, 1762," indicating the beginning of the
church; "Bethel, 1860," the erection of the present house
of worship; "Shiloh, 1865," the coming of the present
pastor; "Salem, 1890," the prosperous completion of the
quarter century. All the lettering was appropriately in
silver.

According to invitation, the following classmates and other associates of the pastor were present to take part in the various exercises of the day, viz:

REV. THOMAS M. CRAWFORD, . . of Delta.
REV. EBENEZER ERSKINE, D. D., . ., . of Newville.
REV. WM. C. CATTELL., D. D., LL. D., . of Philadelphia.
REV. THOS. H. ROBINSON, D. D., { of the Western Theological Seminary, Allegheny, Pa.
REV. WM. M. PAXTON, D. D., LL. D., { of the Theological Seminary, Princeton, N. J.
REV. THOMAS MURPHY, D. D., . . of Philadelphia.

The general subject announced for the morning service was: "*The Christian Church: Her heritage and her responsibility.*" The following was the order of exercises:

ORGAN VOLUNTARY.
DOXOLOGY.
INVOCATION. . . . . . REV. DR. MURPHY.
ANTHEM BY THE CHOIR.—"Praise ye the Lord."—*From*
[*Lambilotte.*
SCRIPTURE READING. . . REV. T. M. CHAWFORD.
HYMN No. 529.—"Oh, where are Kings and Empires now."
PASTOR'S HISTORICAL REVIEW.
ANTHEM BY THE CHOIR.—"How beautiful upon the Mountains."
[*—Perkins.*
ADDRESS. . . . . . DR. T. H. ROBINSON.
ADDRESS. . . . . . DR. WM. M. PAXTON.
PRAYER. . . . . . DR. WM. C. CATTELL.
HYMN No. 585.—"Great Lord of all Thy Churches hear."
BENEDICTION. . . . . . . DR. ERSKINE.

DR. NILES' DISCOURSE.

WENTY-FIVE years of pastoral experience and
Church history reviewed in twenty-five minutes!
Such is the task I have proposed for myself; to
condense into smallest space, records and reminis-
cences which might occupy hours, and even days!
Twenty-five years ago, the circumstances by which we
were environed, and the general condition of American
society were very different from what they are now. Then,
our country was writhing under the agonies of civil war.

Then, the morning papers were read with avidity such as
never before, and the evening bulletins were eagerly watched
to learn what, during another day, had been the movement
of armies, and the results of battle.

Twenty-five years ago, yonder common was surrounded
by hospital wards into which thousands of sick and
wounded from the regiments of different States had been
brought, to receive not only the care of Government officials,
but also the tender ministrations of our kind-hearted, liberal-
handed citizens.

On this very 6th of April, a quarter century ago, the
Army of Virginia was fleeing before the triumphant forces
of Grant; and three days later, their commander, General
Lee, was forced to unconditional surrender. Then, how
the glad news flashed across the continent, and even under
the ocean, till the civilized world felt the thrill of joy! A

few days later, (April 14th) the fourth anniversary of the fall
of Fort Sumter was signalized by raising again the stars
and stripes over the ruins of that historic fortress. On the
evening of that day, when our country was aglow with
enthusiasm, parades and illuminations, the Presbytery of
Harrisburg assembled in this church for its semi-annual
session. It was opened with a sermon by our brother, DR.
ROBINSON, who was then associate pastor with the venerable
DR. DEWITT, at Harrisburg. Amid the felicitations of that
hour, little did we imagine what a night would bring forth!
Little were we prepared for the startling announcement
which came to us next morning (April 15th) of the
assassination of the beloved LINCOLN, and of the reign of
terror which bloody conspirators had produced at Washington! When Presbytery came together that Saturday,
how ardently we hoped that the report might prove to be
exaggerated! How earnestly we prayed that, if possible,
the cup might pass from us, and the Nation's President
live! But, before noon, our worst fears were confirmed;
and so, instead of emblems of joy for the services of the
coming day, these walls that afternoon, like public and
private buildings generally, were festooned with draperies
of mourning! My journal for that Sabbath says: "This
would have been a delightful day, but for the shadow of
awful crime and a great national affliction."

At the morning service, REV. Mr. STERLING, of Williamsport, preached an appropriate sermon, after which the
beloved DAVID E. SMALL, who, a few days previous, had
been elected ruling elder, was formally ordained to that
office by the REV. DR. DEWITT. In the afternoon, a children's meeting was held, in which members of Presbytery,
Messrs. MORE, MILLER, LONG, STERLING and WING,

together with our veteran superintendent, DR. KERR, took part.

The evening service was appointed for my installation, when the sermon was preached by DR. WING, charge to the pastor by DR. DEWITT, and charge to the people, by MR. STERLING. Then at the close of service, what cordial hand-shakings and words of cheerful encouragement! Was minister ever blessed with nobler welcome than was given by those well remembered ones who flocked around this altar! But where are they now? Those members of the session, HENRY M. MCCLELLAN, SAMUEL SMALL, JAMES W. KERR and DAVID E. SMALL! And that remarkable company of trustees, prominent, influential men who attended to "the outward business of the House of God," EDWARD CHAPIN, ELI LEWIS, PHILIP A. SMALL, JOHN EVANS, HENRY WELSH and SAMUEL SMALL! Every one of them gone! Others too, who were called, one after another, to take the offices from which these were successively removed by death! And besides them, many more, noble men and saintly women who loved the gates of Zion, and prayed and labored for her increase. The workers have been changing, but *the work goes on.* Thank God, the foundations of His Church are on the Eternal Rock. His promises for her perpetuity and prosperity and increasing power, are signally fulfilled!

The Presbytery of Harrisburg was a comparatively small body, included in the Synod of Pennsylvania, and connected with the New School branch of the Church. But though few in numbers, it was confessedly large in activities and general influence, and its meetings were occasions of rarely delightful social and spiritual intercourse. When the two great branches of the Presbyterian family came together in the blessed reunion of 1870, this York church, by reason of

its geographical position, became included in the new
Presbytery of Westminster. But it was no union with
strange brethren, to which we then reluctantly submitted.
On the contrary, everything was done to make us feel a
cordial welcome. From the beginning, we found warm
hearts ready to greet us, and fraternal confidence ready to
assure us, and during all succeeding years, even up to these
days of Revision discussion, and honest differences of
opinion, nothing has occurred to make us feel that we were
not one with our brethren in all the essentials of Christian
Fellowship! Owing to the origin and traditions of the early
settlers in York, Presbyterianism is not indigenous to this
soil, and could not flourish here, as in other parts of the
State, where the limitations were not so restrictive! But,
as an exotic it has gradually become acclimated, and its
growth increasingly vigorous. We can hardly realize now,
how few the numbers and how embarrassing the circumstances of those who made the beginnings here, more than
a hundred years ago. But obstacles and discouragements
with which Dr. CATHCART, the first pastor, and his faithful
supporters had to contend, were much reduced, as time went
on, in the experience of his successors, WALLACE and
EMERSON, HUTCHINS and STREET. At the commencement
of this pastorate, of the 115 communicants in the church,
only 22 were males, and scarcely a single member under
twenty years of age. Now, of the 457 attending members,
135 are males, and of these, a goodly proportion (30 or 40)
young men and boys. Of course these must be judged
charitably and nursed tenderly, for they have the volatility
of youth, and are subject to its temptations, but thank God,
we have peculiar facilities for their Christian culture—
facilities which they seem glad to improve! Years of happy
spiritual development, we trust, are before them, years of

enlarged activity and spirituality and usefulness in the Master's service.

Some of the best experiences of my life have been in laboring with and for *young people*. They are comparatively free from the deadening, restrictive influence of old habits, and on *them*, must be the hope of the Church. From my first Sabbath in York, when the superintendent, DR. KERR, invited me to visit the school, and rising to their feet, the whole company gave me a greeting in beautiful words written for the purpose:

" Welcome Pastor! Welcome Brother!
One and all, we welcome thee!"

from that memorable day down to the present, I have had much encouragement in dealing with the young. Within a month from that date, inquiry meetings began to be held, which were marked by undoubted tokens of the Holy Spirit's presence. Among these was a service unique and impressive, which some of you well remember, held in the yet unfurnished kitchen of the old parsonage. It was a singular place, chosen for the quiet that reigned there, but around it we may well believe, the angels of God hovered with joyful interest, as they saw that it was the birthplace of precious souls! Here too, should be noticed the opening of another spring of blessed influences, the *Ladies' Prayer Meeting*,—commenced by two congenial spirits, in a little room in the Washington House, while yet the pastor's family were waiting there till the arrival of our goods. Accessions to this band of praying ones were gradually made, and through all the years, it has continued to send out a stream of spiritual life which has flowed into all the channels of the church's activity. Who shall tell how those who thus waited together around

that altar of social worship, have gained selectest blessings
for the Church ; and how often to their sensitive, spiritual
perceptions, has been indicated the first sound of a "going
in the tops of the mulberry trees," token that the Lord was
coming to visit His people! O! those precious seasons of
quickened religious interest which we have enjoyed in
answer to prayer, when Christians came together under a
fresh baptism of the Holy Ghost, and when converts were
added to the Church ! During this whole quarter century,
scarcely a communion service without more or less accessions being made to our number. At the first June communion, among those who came forward publicly to
acknowledge Christ, were some who now are scattered far
and wide over the earth, and some who have gone to
Heaven ; but others there were, who yet remain, active,
useful and beloved, two of them now trustees in the
church. In the next year (1866), forty-seven candidates
were received by confession ; included among whom were
two *boys*, sons of elders who had been praying earnestly
for them, and who rejoiced, O so heartily ! when we welcomed them to the Lord's Table ! Now, each of those
sons has come to the responsibilities of manhood, filling
just the offices held by his father,—each one an elder in
the church, and a trustee of the congregation ! Verily,
God is faithful to His covenant. "The children of Thy
servants shall continue, and their seed shall be established
before Thee ! " Again, in '67 and '68 we were blessed
with encouraging fruits, and so in each succeeding year
down to the present, additions varying from twenty-five to
fifty and sixty annually. At different times, I have been
favored with visits and help from brethren beloved :—DRS.
TAYLOR, DURYEA, PIERSON, HERALD and others, and in
common with other churches of this city, we have shared

the labors of such men as HAMMOND, MOODY and MUN-
HALL. But in everything our sufficiency was of God, and
to Him be all the praise. Summing up the whole, *nearly
a thousand different persons* have been in the church for a
longer or shorter time, under my pastoral care. To many
of them I administered the baptismal seal in their infancy,
over them I watched, through childhood, taught them
in the inquiry room, received them to the communion!
Others came with letters from sister churches, and were
welcomed in the name of the Lord. Some I have married, some I have ministered to in sickness, and some I
have buried! Some have gone away, and are doing
Christ's service in other fields, and others, thank God,—
more than four hundred faithful ones remain! O, how
many relations, sacred, tender, far-reaching, immeasurable,
has God appointed for a settled pastor! Several of my
brethren, in their letters, speak with admiration and beautiful sympathy, in regard to these relations. I am, more
than ever, deeply impressed with them. Would that in
them all, I had been more wise and faithful, my work better done, my soul ever on fire with zeal for the glory of
Christ and the welfare of souls!

About the time to which I have referred (Feb. 25, 1866),
was inaugurated a movement, one of the first in the land,
the blessed influence of which has been widely felt. I
refer to the *Temperance Society* connected with our Sunday-
school, which must be forever associated with the name of
DAVID E. SMALL, who was, to the end of his life, its only
president, and who did so much by his personal addresses
and his pen, to recommend it to others. Many who have
gone out amid the temptations of life, we know have gratefully referred to the principles and pledges here accepted,

aud many other churches, sending for our constitution, have organized on the same plan.

Here, let me also refer to the *growth of the missionary spirit in our church.* Formerly, the old fashioned monthly concert on Monday evening, was sustained by a little number who were not willing to be out of harmony with others who thus met regularly to confer and pray in reference to the progress of Christ's kingdom. But, after that concert was changed to take the place of the first *Wednesday* evening in each month, and reporters were appointed for the principal mission fields, the interest began to increase. Gradually, new agencies were instituted : " THE WOMAN'S FOREIGN MISSIONARY SOCIETY," " THE NILES MISSION BAND," for young ladies, and " THE ALWAYS READY BAND " for little girls. Likewise, " THE WOMAN'S HOME MISSIONARY SOCIETY," " THE WESTMINSTER HOME MISSION BAND," etc., through all which, wider interest has been developed, until now, in common with others, we wonder what would become of the great missionary work, except for the consecrated love and zeal of the Marthas, and Lydias, and Priscillas in our churches.

I have referred to coincidences. Another one of special interest should be noticed. On communion day, March 3rd, '78, two twin brothers, whom I had baptized in infancy, were, when twelve years of age, publicly received into full communion with the Church, and at the same time, two other twin boys, who had been nurtured in our Sunday-school, were received. Now, the four are active soldiers in the sacramental host, one pair among the most prompt and regular and reliable supporters of this church in which they were born. The other pair, having passed through a full course of academic and theological education, are now serving Christ with marked success as home missionaries

in Dakota. For such fruits of his ministry, any pastor has
especial reason for thanksgiving to God! Others there are
of whom it would be pleasant to speak,—once among us,
cherished and beloved, who now, in professional and business circles, are letting their light shine, and some, who, as
wives of ministers and prominent laymen, are, in widely
different spheres, transmitting the sacred influences here
received.

In October, '83, *twenty-six* of our members went forth to
form the nucleus of what has now become the vigorous
" Calvary Presbyterian Church," in a growing part of the
city; and in '87 *thirty-eight* more were dismissed to form
the " Westminster Church," which is doing good work in
another direction. We felt the loss of those brethren and
sisters, excellent and beloved. We have missed their presence in our assemblies, but we believe that they went forth
in the name and with the spirit of the Master. We thank
God for their successes, and we pray that His smile may be
upon them continually. Some of them are here to-day
and we bid them hearty welcome, as they have come back
to join with us in these services of remembrance and
praise!

Going back to 1867, some of you will remember that
cold Sabbath (31st) in March, when we gathered for the
last time, in the old lecture-room, before it was demolished
to give place for the present chapel; and when we sang:

> " With smiling hope, yet tearful eye
> Dear old Sunday-school room, good-bye! "

When the new building was finished it seemed ample for
our needs, though now it begins to be, like its humble pred-
ecessor, too strait for our growing numbers! It was dedi-
cated May 24th, '68 : REV. DR. DURYEA, then of Brooklyn,

Rev. Mr. Emerson, a former pastor, Hon. Linus Child, of Boston, and others taking part in the service. In that chapel, and in this loved sanctuary, what varied scenes of spiritual privilege and power have we witnessed through the passing years! and how many hallowed associations are centered there! Dear to memory are those early morning prayer-meetings, conducted by different brethren successively, in the spring of '68, and the happy spiritual results that were manifest. And you remember that notable gathering, which proved to be the last meeting of the Synod of Pennsylvania, N. S., when you formed so many pleasant acquaintances with brethren from abroad, and saw such winning exhibitions of the fellowship of kindred minds. Of various meetings of Presbytery which have been held here, I should like also to speak, and of that annual Feast of Love, so long maintained by the churches of York in observance of "*The Week of Prayer.*" It was highly appreciated by many earnest souls, and it tended greatly to foster that spirit of Christian charity beautifully expressed by one of our departed saints. "Nero, the bloody tyrant," (she said,) "wished that the people of Rome had *one neck!* In such a wish I could sympathize with him, but not for the same reason! He wished all the Romans so united that he might cut off their heads by a single stroke! But, if all the Christians of York had one neck, I should like to put my arms around it, and thus show how *I love them all!*"

This suggests a thought in regard to the *style of Christian character* which has been produced among us, through the years. Not all that could have been desired, by far! Not that, in many cases, our hopes have been realized, or that we have been spared the grief and shame and reproach which a church must endure when any of her members prove backsliders and unfaithful. But, on the other hand,

I am sure there have been many here, evidently called of
God, and endued with power for His service.

As I pass up and down along the corridors of the past,
there rise before me men of rare gifts and consecrated
influence, whose words of prayer and praise still echo from
these walls, and whose works of faith and love still follow
in lines of blessing all around. Those *model elders*, like
John the Beloved, and James the Just, and Paul the Faithful, and Barnabas the son of Consolation, who went with
me, from house to house, labored with me in the inquiry
meetings, and with me, welcomed new-comers to the
Eucharistic Feast. And "those women who labored with
me in the Gospel," like Mary and Martha, and "the elect
Lady " to whom the Apostle wrote: "Dear departed ones!"
who were, as *you*, Beloved, are now, "my Hope and Joy,
and Crown of Rejoicing!" Who shall say that *they* are not
here to-day, invisible witnesses of what we do! Who shall
say that we are not "compassed about" with a great cloud
of sympathizing spirits who rejoice to see that the work is
going on—that such an amount of rising talent and varied
activities and earnest purpose is consecrated to the service which they loved! Yes, glorified ones! we remember
you, with grateful hearts! and we would follow you,
wherein you followed Christ, until, like you, we shall have
accomplished our day, and shall enter on the Heavenly
rest!

It is time to stop. But there are some other words my
heart requires me to speak. Beloved! you have dealt very
kindly with me, all the way, and are doing so still. You
have borne with my infirmities, you have lightened my
burdens, you have done very much to stay up my hands
and encourage my heart. In joy and in sorrow, in health
and in sickness, to me and to mine, you have been sympa-

thizing helpers and endeared personal friends. Ever prompt
in the discharge of pecuniary obligations, you have also
abounded in *voluntary* expressions of thoughtful regard.
Your holiday gifts and other frequent tokens of affection,
your generous provision for that European trip, which
proved so great a benefit to me in many respects, and of
late, emphatically, your liberal movement in erecting that
commodious parsonage home, fit complement to the other
church property not only, but essential to the comfort and
health alike of myself and of her who has shared all my
experiences and whose love for the church has no bounds,
all these things I desire distinctly and gratefully to recount.
Giving regularly for various objects of Christian benevolence
abroad, you have also remembered the deeds of beneficence
at home.* Being ministered unto, you have been careful
to minister. You have shown that it is no unmeaning form
of words, used in the settlement of a pastor, when he is
promised " whatever may be needful for the honor of
religion, and for his competent worldly maintenance."

When I came to this place, it was as to a strange country,
and by no planning or previous desire of my own. It
verily seemed as if the Lord had opened the way, and that
He did not intend I should go anywhere else! So, through
the years, it has, ever since, seemed. As for the future, it
is for Him to decide. So long as He appoint, I shall be at
your service. My time, talents, education, experience,
mental and spiritual strength, whatever I have, shall be
cheerfully used according to His direction!

But there is a side of the picture we have been consider-
ing which I cannot view with satisfaction. It is enough to

* During the period under review, this congregation has given to the Boards of
the Presbyterian Church, and other causes of charity, not less than $108,000: and
for all purposes, congregational and benevolent, about $239,000.

startle, and to make me humble. Such a review of what is
irrevocably past, *seems very much like Judgment Day work!*
It suggests what might have been! O, that I had been more
vigilant and active and prayerful and consecrated to this
great work! I wish I had done more, with the help of God,
to make me worthy of your confidence and love. I wish
I deserved all the kind things which brethren, far and near,
are speaking and writing about me! But there is no recall
nor reconstruction of what is past. I can only trust in
abounding grace; grace to pardon all my short comings;
grace to counteract my mistakes; grace to accept and bless
what I have tried to do in the Master's name; grace to
sanctify and guide in the days to come. I believe in
unlimited possibilities for a faithful pastor, and an earnest,
united people. I shall be, in the future, *very much what you
shall help me to be!* Your prayers can invoke for me
Divine aid, your sympathies can make me strong, your love
infuse new life into my heart pulsations, your co-operation
ensure my enlarged success. In this confidence let me
repose. And, "may the grace of our Lord Jesus Christ be
with us all. Amen!"

DR. ROBINSON'S ADDRESS.

"The Christian Church : her heritage received from the fathers, and
her consequent responsibility."

IT is well for us when, like Bunyan's pilgrim, we have
reached on our life journey, the summit of some
Delectable Mountain, to look back along the way
over which we have come, and where too, may still,
be seen the footprints of earlier walkers; and to look forward also, to catch, if we may, some cheering glimpses of
that City of God to which all loyal hearts incessantly turn.
We look backward that we may gather inspiration for the
more hopeful and courageous onward look. We look back
that we may see more clearly how our rich and happy
present sprung out of the past, and how the better time
coming will be but the inevitable outcome of the forces we
are using to-day. We are the heirs of other generations.
But a few years ago entered we upon our large possessions.
We may have enriched and enlarged them, but it was not
as paupers we began our lives. We trade upon the capital
of the past. We carry on the labors which other men
started and take up what other men laid down. We reap
in fields that were sowed and watered by many preceding
generations. God laid upon many of his faithful ones in
the past a long and painful apprenticeship, during which
they toiled much and received little, often but the bread
and water of affliction. The spoils of their long conflict

are heaped about us. The good seed sown in tears is now
shedding a heavenly fragrance around our lives. Some of
it may yet blossom and bear fruit over our graves. We
cannot separate ourselves from our sires. The passing
ages keep up a running account, and the latest generation
is always the heaviest debtor. What we get from the past
we are bound to hand over to the future with usury. Woe
to us if there be any default in the payment.

What a heritage we have in the noble men of all the past.
All Christly lives are ours that were ever lived under the
sun. We are not hampered by any lines of race or nation
or church. No Babel confusion of sects shall hinder our
unity with every member of the large and growing Chris-
tendom. Our doors open of their own accord to receive
all out of whose lives something of the Infinite love
shines. It matters not whether they worship in cathedral,
with stately ceremonial and solemn chant, or in some humble conventicle, with simple rites and holy psalm. · We
cleave to the Apostolic succession of godly men. They
are our ancestry everywhere. We rejoice to recognize the
features of Jesus anywhere, and his followers shall never
be alien to our hearts.

Yet with that broader Catholic spirit that embraces people of every name and place and age whose lives are hid
with Christ in God, we confess a peculiar attachment to
those special forms of our common Christianity that
hereditary descent and family training, and life-long com-
panionship have made familiar and a part of ourselves.
We love that Presbyterianism "whose seed is in itself
after its kind." We recall with elation of soul, its history.
We trace our genealogy in its annals. We feel its blood
throbbing in our veins, its iron in our wills. We make
no comparisons between it and other forms of Christian

faith. We assert for it no superiority. We do not fail to
remember how the goodness and purity of it have again
and again been tarnished, how it has once and again failed
to meet the demands of the hour. Yet we have a heritage
of our own. We have a history that runs along its own
lines. We look back upon men and events and institutions and policies, upon a great literature, upon a theology
upon form of Christian work, upon great enterprizes that
are peculiarly our own. There are things from the past
which have come into our possession and keeping—they
are the things who under God have moulded us, made us
the people we are, fashioned our churches, inspired our
beliefs, and shaped our lives. The power we have for the
world's uplifting, our influence upon the family, society,
the state for good or ill, what we are to Humanity, what
we are for Christ, cannot be separated from the mould, the
spirit, the substance of our Presbyterianism. We may
well remind ourselves often of all in the past that is peculiarly our own. We may recall the fact that ere the ses-
sions of that memorable assembly of learned divines and
eminent statesmen, who were summoned in 1643 to meet
in the chapel of Henry VII and construct our standards
of doctrine and polity, had closed their session, the eyes
and thoughts of many of its members had turned to this
continent beyond the sea as the home of a future Church.
Seventy of its members approved a plan of sending colo-
nies of their church members to settle in America. The
plan failed for the hour, but later the seeds of Westminster
were wafted hither and took deep, strong root in American
soil.

What a heritage of Christian song has come down to us
through the ages! From that Redemption Hymn of
Israel by the Red Sea, when the voice of the Church of

God first became audible, down to the present, one generation has carried on to another the accents of holy song.
David, from the sheepfold and from the throne, led the Old
Testament harmonies. The Magnificat of the blessed vir-
gin Mary, mother of Jesus, began the hymnology of the
New Testament. That Matin song of Christianity lifted
the Name that is above every name, and taught the singers
of each succeeding age. And what singers the Church has
had in all the Christian centuries! And they with their
songs are all ours to-day! Ambrose, filling the streets of
Milan with the praises of Christ; Gregory calling down in
sacred song the celestial fire of the Holy Ghost: "Come,
O Creator Spirit, come!" Bernard, hailing in immortal
verse, the "Sacred Head once wounded;" Luther giving
the German people their hymn-book, as well as their
Bible; Wesley guiding the feet of generations to the Rock
of Ages; Cowper pointing us to the fountain where all
sins are washed away; and Watts and Newton and Keble
and Palmer, and the great choir of priestly singers who
with sweet and joyous, or with deep and touching hymns
have borne the heart of the Church heavenward; what a
priceless heritage in these songs that never grow old!

- The little Presbytery of Harrisburg which a quarter of
a century ago installed our brother as pastor over this
church of York, was born when storms were sweeping
over the Presbyterianism of this country. The Presbytery
of Carlisle out of which it sprung, lay in the very heart of
the great Scotch-Irish settlement that filled this region.
The people and their pastors were all alike original and
thorough Presbyterians of the stricter sort. They were
averse to change and abhorred all speculations in theology.
Their thoughts, traditions and faith, their plans and hopes
and fears, and modes of Christian work were everywhere

the same. They were the worthy descendants of those
good men and true who in the earliest days had poured in
hither in streams of immigration and planted their homes
along the very borders of a savage wilderness. They came
with Bibles, confessions, catechisms, with an ordained and
learned ministry with ruling elders, ready for church
organizations and all the forms and activities of both private and public Christian life. The home, the school and
the church rose side by side. Nowhere was education
more universal. In no land upon the face of the earth,
save perhaps the land from which most of them came, was
the Bible more the book of the home, and nowhere was
there a greater proportion of homes that were intelligent
and heartily and openly religious. They were at the first
and for many years, a universally sanctuary-going and
sanctuary-loving people. Their manners were simple.
Domestic virtues abounded. They were sound in the faith,
sober in mind, frugal and thrifty in their habits, intense in
their love of civil and religious liberties, loyal and law-
abiding, but ready and bold to withstand oppression and
resist wrong. They filled these valleys with the fruits of
physical, intellectual and Christian culture. What length-
ened rolls of renowned and sainted men, ministers and laymen, might be written from the days of ANDERSON and
THOMPSON and ELDER, and the CRAIGHEADS, down to the
later days with our own memories of CATHCART, and
CREIGH and HARPER and DEWITT.

It might have been supposed that when trouble came
such a class of people would stand together. And they
did so for the most part. It was but a meager handful
that went forth from the parent church in this region : but
four churches of any special strength in a country stretch-
ing along the Susquehanna for one hundred and thirty

miles. It required courage of the highest kind, the deepest convictions and the purest motives for that small and
scattered minority to go forth and stand so lonely amid a
great mass of sister churches with whom they had shared
the closest fellowship for half a century and more. Into
the causes of that separation it is not necessary to enter.
Enough to say, the men that formed that little Presbytery
had no new and strange theology to defend, no changes in
church order to propose, no new forms of church worship
or new measures of church work to present. They were
like their brethren about them. They only felt that a
wrong had been done against which they could protest in
no other and better way, and they went forth to live and
believe, to work and to preach as they had been wont to
do for years.

For nearly the third of a century these few and scattered
churches and their pastors wrought on, until the grass had
grown green over the old battle-fields, the war cries had
ceased, and the memories of past strifes had nearly faded
away.

Christian affections had meanwhile been reasserting
themselves. Hands had reached across the narrow lines
of separation. Theological affinities were too strong for
resistance. The children of the early and common household could not stay apart, and twenty years ago they came
together to find that the spirit and the faith of the same
ancestry lived equally in them all.

When, thirty-six years ago, the hand of a gracious Provi-
dence drew me to this favored region where five generations
of my ancestry had lived, and where some of them were
laid to rest, my lot was cast in this little Presbytery of
Harrisburg. Some of its founders, the solid and scholarly
KENNEDY of Welch-Run Church, and the venerable and

beloved CATHCART of this church, had passed away full of honors. Of other men who were with them and continued for years in the care of the churches, I may say a few words. The smallness of the Presbytery and its peculiar position amid a greatly preponderating number of Old School churches, tended to knit pastors and churches in bonds of strong and endearing friendship. We felt our loneliness and clung to each other with the greater tenacity. We visited each other's houses and churches as personal friends and as brothers for friendly, household greetings. We welcomed each other's faces and clasped each other's hands with something deeper than denominational courtesy. We assisted each other at communions and in revivals with a tender family affection. We were not fellow-Presbyters : we were brothers, and our Presbyterial meetings were far more social than ecclesiastical. We conferred and prayed together with a personal, rather than an official spirit. We talked rather than debated. Formality and stateliness were banished. Our long rides together in visits to the smaller and feebler churches hidden away in the valleys, the welcomes that were received and given, the days that we contrived to spend together in religious exercises and brotherly conferences, the unreserve, the genial warmth, the tender queries about each other's homes and churches and labors made our little Presbytery a brotherhood, rather than an ecclesiastical court. There was no room for rivalries. Jealousies were unknown. The generous regard for each other was as touching as it was beautiful. And when the time came to dissolve our little brotherhood and to send its churches here and there, and its nine ministers into five new and larger and separate Presbyteries, where they would but seldom again greet each other, there were hidden tears and quiet heart-achings that others wot little of!

It is a joy to speak of these men and recall their goodly
lives. STERLING, of Williamsport, gone home to God, so
kindly and open-hearted, so liberal in judgment, so earnest
in preaching, so devoted in life; DeWITT of Harrisburg,
my colleague for thirteen years, so impressive in personal
presence, so unquestioned in pulpit power, so finished as a
writer, and so conservative and sound in theology ; the
beloved DR. WING, of Carlisle, who united to a pure heart
and guileless spirit and gentlest manners, an intellect so
clear, a mind so stored with rich and varied learning, and
powers of attractive presentation of truth surpassed by few
of his generation. Nor these men only! What noble and
ever-to-be-remembered men we had in the ruling eldership
of our churches, men worthy to stand by the best of
pastors as counsellors and ensamples to the flock: JOHN
B. HALL, of Williamsport, and PETER WILSON, of Spring
Mills, men of unflinching faith and irreproachable life, and
unending goodness; JAMES W. and JOHN A. WEIR,
brothers in blood, and heroes in service ; the first a Nestor
in wisdom, a prince both in prayers and alms, a captain
among the elect; the second, an apostle of love, a Barnabas
in consolation, a child in his guileless qualities for Christ's
Kingdom.   `

And in this church, for many years, among other excellent
men there were these who especially attracted my admiration, and won my heart: Dr. H. M. McCLELLAN, quick,
thoughtful, sagacious, true in judgment; Dr. JAMES W.
KERR, impulsive in noble ways, inspiring in his enthusiasm,
sanguine in his hopes, large in charities of heart and
charities of life ; SAMUEL SMALL, so calm and self-poised, so
gentlemanly in his bearing, so unwearied in service, so
princely in heart and hand; DAVID E. SMALL, so broad-
minded and high-hearted, so full of divine fire that the

coldest natures felt the warmth of his sympathetic presence
and admired his loyalty to Christ and the Church.

As memory busies itself in recalling the men and scenes
of the past, the everlasting friendships formed with good
men, who by their counsels kept our wayward feet upon the
track divine; the glad revivals where together we rejoiced
over sinners coming home to God; the happy gathering of
brethren in the ministry and the eldership where we were
sure of loving recognition and Christian fellowship, I cannot cease to congratulate myself that so large a part of my
life was spent amid so excellent environments: and congratulate my brother also, that he too, was led hither by a
Gracious Hand, and has spent so many years among the
good and enduring things of this region that God has per-
petually blessed.

Following Dr. Robinson, Rev. Dr. Paxton made some
felicitous remarks in regard to the history of Presbyterianism in this region, going back to the early days when his
own grandfather was the only minister of our denomination
in that part of the original York county which is now known
as Adams county, and Dr. Cathcart, his contemporary,
was the only one in this county. His descriptions of the
long and faithful labors of these worthy men, and of the
influence which they exerted far and wide for moulding
the character of Christian people in this extended region,
were very interesting and instructive.

The exercises of this morning service were closed with
prayer by Rev. Dr. Cattell.

CHILDREN'S SERVICE.

IN the afternoon at one o'clock, the Primary Department of the Sunday-school, assembled in the usual place in the chapel, which had just been enlarged and beautified and newly furnished. Many parents and friends of the little ones were also present, and an air of festive gladness seemed to be felt by every one. Brief addresses to the school were made by Messrs CRAWFORD and CATTELL, and the scholars gave some of their recitations and songs.

YOUNG PEOPLE'S SERVICES.

At two o'clock the other departments of the school, together with the Young People's Society of Christian Endeavor, and a goodly portion of the congregation filled the church, where the following exercises were held under direction of the superintendent, ELDER JOHN M. BROWN:

1. Anthem by the choir.
2. Remarks by DR. NILES, describing his introduction to the Sunday-school twenty-five years ago, in the little frame building where it then met; recalling the names of certain who then were scholars, but now, some are teachers, some are parents of scholars, some are laboring elsewhere, and some have gone to Heaven.
3. Prayer by the Superintendent.
4. Hymn—"I hope to meet you all."
5. Remarks by JOHN H. SMALL, Jr., President of the Y.

P. S. C. E., in which he sketched the origin, object and
wonderful growth through the country of this training-
school of the church. In this church the society has over
100 members, and it is steadily increasing in numbers and
usefulness.

    6. Hymn—" Harvest Time."
    7. Remarks by DRS. ERSKINE, CATTELL and PAXTON.
    8. Hymn—" Go labor on."
    9. Prayer by DR. MURPHY.
    10. Benediction.

The following is a summary of

DR. ERSKINE'S REMARKS.

"The three great instrumentalities for the religious
instruction of the young, are the home, the school and the
church. The father is by divine appointment, the prophet,
priest and king of his household. On him rests the obliga-
tion to see that the family is trained up in the knowledge,
worship and service of God.

"The first great religous truth impressed upon the mind
of Presbyterian youth is the answer to the question,
' What is the chief end of man ? ' This answer has contributed much to form the character and guide the lives of
our people. Sir William Hamilton, the noted Scottish
philosopher, has said that ' the great end of man is man.'
These two statements will be seen to harmonize perfectly,
the moment we realize that the more fully we are developed
physically, intellectually, morally and spiritually, the more
of an honor will we be to our Creator, and the more praise
will we bring to His great name.

"God's glory is the end of all things. We glorify God in
proportion as we make Him known. He rolled the planets

upon their orbits, that He might make known His natural
perfections—His wisdom, goodness and power.   He made
man in His own image, in knowledge, righteousness and
holiness, that we might reflect His own moral attributes—
His holiness, justice, goodness and truth.   He permitted
man as a free moral agent to be tempted and to fall, and
overruled it to His greater glory in the redemptive work
of the Lord Jesus Christ.   God's character and perfections
and will were more fully revealed in the Book of Divine
Revelation and in the person, character, life, death and
resurection of the Lord Jesus Christ.   Nowhere in all the
universe has there been such a discovery of the Divine
perfections as in the life and character of the Son of God
Incarnate.   All moral perfections are revealed in Him, and
a flood of divine glory was poured forth upon the cross.
To this cross all the historic lines of previous dispensations
converge.   From it all subsequent historic lines irradiate.

"The great aim of a religious education should be to
restore in us the image of God, and to secure for each
department of our nature the highest possible strength and
development.

"1. The first and lowest part of our nature to be trained
for the activities of life is our physical or bodily nature.
There is not a limb or faculty of the body but has its
office.   Nothing is superfluous.   Every limb or member
should therefore be most religiously preserved and strengh-
ened.   This is what has been called muscular Christianity.
The importance of a sound mind in a sound body had a
high place among the ancients.   Our modern sports and
gymnasiums are designed to meet the wants of the young
in this respect.   These are all well enough, provided they
are not allowed to run to excess.   We are not to put that
highest which God has put lowest.   Let the physical health

and strength of our youth be preserved. Let the best
methods to secure this result be employed. Let them, like
the ancient athletes and the modern combatants, be put
under a strict regimen as to diet, exercise, and as to all
that will intoxicate. Let right habits in all respects be
formed and sustained. Let our youth beware of indolence
which relaxes all the energies. Let them shun the vices
which are most expensive and destructive of all the vital
forces. The best laws of health and happiness are the Ten
Commandments. Let all our scholars know and take heed
to what is required and forbidden in them. The weakness
of our present Christianity is the lack of a high standard of
morality. Reproach has been cast upon the Sabbath-
school in some quarters, by reason of the number of those
connected with it who have fallen into gross crimes.

"2. The second part of our nature calling for education is
the intellect. To secure this is the chief if not the exclusive
aim of too many of our schools and colleges. Their aim
is to develop and sharpen the intellectual faculties, the per-
ceptive and the reflective: the reason, the memory, the
judgment and the imagination. The tendency to overestimate the importance of intellectual culture to the
neglect of moral and spiritual development, makes it all
the more important that the moral and spiritual nature
should receive the most careful and assiduous training in
the Sabbath-school and the Church, if our youth are to be
prepared for the great battle of life. Right moral principles
must be inculcated upon our youth. The precepts of the
moral law should be deeply impressed upon them from
childhood up. Right moral habits should be enforced
upon all the members of the household. The children
should be taught to know God and to exercise toward
Him, from their earliest childhood, a reverential and filial

fear. They should be trained to habits of truthfulness, honesty, temperance and chastity, as in His presence from the earliest period of their youth.

"3. But when thus trained physically, intellectually and morally, if their spiritual natures are suffered to remain undeveloped, they must signally fail to attain the great end of human existence. The first great need of all is to learn their true condition in relation to God and the life to come. The fact of the fall, and of the general spiritual wreck and ruin of the race, and of the absolute necessity of the new birth, are fundamental truths in all religious training. Except we are born again we cannot see the kingdom of God. It is only the regenerate that come to a saving knowledge of Christ, and to the exercise of true faith in Him. It is only such that live a holy life and are saved. To bring us thus to the knowledge, image, favor and communion of God, is the great end of the training of the Sabbath-school and of the Church.

"The great instrumentalities in order to this religious training, are the Bible, the catechisms of the Church, and a sound Christian literature. The Bible is the text-book. Presbyterians have well been characterized by Green, the English historian, as 'the people of a book, and that book is the Bible.' And 'their religion,' said Carlisle, 'was the chief fact about them." Then no one can overestimate the indebtedness of our Church to the Shorter Catechism. It has given to our people definite knowledge as to the fundamental truths of Christianity. It has made them a stable people in the midst of all the fluctuations of religious opinions about them. It has been to them a declaration of the things most surely believed among us. It has served as a protest against error. It has proved a bond of union and a means of instruction and growth. Such, then,

teachers and scholars, and all that are here assembled, is
the fourfold education which we all need.   This alone will
fit us for the highest usefulness here, and for the greatest.
happiness hereafter."

———‡o‡———

DR. CATTELL followed in an address sparkling with
humor and freighted with words of wise counsel to the
young, and he in like manner was succeeded by DR.
PAXTON who spoke with impressive effect upon "the *stuff*"
of which successful men are made.

Both addresses were much enjoyed by the whole congregation, old and young, and we greatly regret that they
cannot be reproduced in full.

SUNDAY EVENING,
SEVEN O'CLOCK.

Union Services with the Calvary and Westminster Churches.
General Subject:—THE PASTORAL OFFICE,—ITS NATURE,
RELATIONS AND INFLUENCE.

HE church was crowded in every part, and to the end intense interest in the exercises was manifested. The choir rendered the "Te Deum in C,"—*Shyrock.* The Scripture Lesson was read by REV. WIL- MER McNAIR, pastor of the Westminster Church.

DR. ERSKINE led in prayer, after which DR. MURPHY spoke with impressive effect on *Hereditary Influence,*—a subject, he said, intimately connected with that which had been announced.

DR. MURPHY'S ADDRESS.

"Hereditary influence is a fact of surpassing practical importance. It is bound up with God's covenant with His church and people, and it has such splendid illustra- tion in the anniversary events of this day and evening, that we ought not to fail of giving it careful consideration.

"The influences, the blessed fruits of which we see in the grand history of this church, this faithful pastor, this earnest congregation, and these brethren who were associ- ated in theological study so long ago, had their spring at

least two hundred years before, and they are still going on
with ever renewed vigor. Their very first trace we find
from a woman, blessed and faithful—a woman whose name
even was not, until very recently, found on any printed
page. To her, more than to any other human being, our
church is indebted. To her, an humble girl in the north
of Ireland, we are to trace back the influences, one splendid
branch of which, out of tens of thousands, we are very
justly admiring to-day. Her name, but recently discovered
in the records of the court of Bucks county, found there on
a deed—the name of CATHARINE KENNEDY, should find a
most honored place in the history of our Church.

"Unseen, unheralded, almost unknown, her influence was
deeper, stronger, wider and more lasting than any other in
our annals. An Irish girl, brought up in a Presbyterian
manse in an atmosphere of religion, her mind stored with
sacred truth, she could not probably remember the time
when she did not supremely love her God. God was pre-
paring her for a life record probably equalled by that of
no other human being in influence for weal on this land.
A finer instance the world has hardly ever beheld of uncon-
scious influence.

"She was married in 1702 to a young Episcopal clergy-
man recently graduated from Trinity College in Dublin, of
fine mental endowments and culture. How much had she
to do through her godly example and refined tact in leading
him to leave the Church of his fathers and enter that of the
Presbyterian name? How much in establishing him in
the doctrines and order of his adopted faith?

"A few years are passed in their native country, part of
the time in County Amagh, and part in Coleraine, County
Antrim. Four sons are born to them, Gilbert, and William, and John, and Charles. With no permanent settle-

ment for them at home, and an increasing family to be
educated, an earnest call came for missionaries in America.
Shall they go? Who can tell how much the godly wife's
devotion to the cause of Christ, her maternal care for the
future of her boys, and her strong, earnest, sanctified good
sense had to do with bringing her husband, the REV. WM.
TENNENT to this land? They reach it, but only to find it
a little removed from an absolute wilderness. How much
had her patient endurance and comforting words to do with
cheering her sometimes desponding husband in those trying
days!

"The Log College is founded. Where was she then?
Would it ever have been built without her counsel, her
cheer and her self-sacrifice? And now we see her in her
best estate—her husband to encourage, her family to sus-
tain by her careful economy, new boys to receive into her
household as students of the school, or to provide for them
in the neighborhood. We fancy all these boys coming to
her as to a mother, telling her of their doubts and fears and
looking to her for advice in all their troubles. She receives
them, too, into her motherly confidence, cheers them in
their homesickness, nurses them in their ailments, counsels
them in difficulties.

"Brave Catharine! thy name is not heralded, but God
knows how much thy tender wisdom contributed to making
the Log College the unspeakable blessing it became to the
Church and to the country!

"But the effects of her influence were only beginning to
be seen there. Would those boys ever have been the great
and good men which they afterwards became, had it not
been for her agency in forming their character? Her daily
care over them, her yearning love for their souls, the
charming power of her godly example, her affectionate

lessons of piety, her exalted Christian principles and her self-control and self-sacrifices—these were unseen influences which she could impart, and which she did impart, with all the tenderness of the woman and the mother. Thus she aided in establishing their deepest and purest principles and rendering the most important assistance in forming their character.

"Afterward they went forth, preaching the gospel in every quarter, bringing thousands of souls to Christ, building up churches in many regions, establishing schools and academies, some of them almost as influential as the one in which they had received their own training for the ministry of the gospel, and starting streams of godly influence that flowed over the whole land, the currents of which have not subsided even to the present day. Nottingham Academy, Faggs Manor, Pequea, Jefferson College, Hampden Sidney College of Virginia, Princeton College and many other institutions are monuments to the power and perseverance of this blessed woman, whom God raised up and graciously led all her days, to leave a sanctifying impress upon our history.

"Where is there another person who originated such chains of godly influences as these? After what she did, who shall claim that they occupy positions too obscure for them to accomplish anything in the great cause of Christ for the redemption of the lost world! Whoever at any time attempts to write the history of the Presbyterian Church in these United States of America, let him give to the name of CATHARINE KENNEDY a place of honor that shall be second to no other, or, rather, let him place it above all the rest.

"Following down the stream of influences which had this humble but most blessed origin, we come next to the ten

Log College evangelists, GILBERT, WILLIAM JR., JOHN and
CHARLES TENNENT, SAMUEL FINLY, SAMUEL and JOHN
BLAIR, WILLIAM ROBINSON, JOHN ROWLAND and CHARLES
C. BEATTY. All these imbibing the earnest evangelical,
and well-trained spirit of the Log College, and each of them
appointed to a different branch of the work, went out to the
glorious calling of spreading the gospel, and sound learning,
and devoted piety over the whole country. And won-
drously was God with them, so that the land received a
new impress from their day forward.

"We next select a simple branch of these influences as
they flowed on and spread abroad, that which was connected
with the preaching of the REV. JOHN ROWLAND, one of the
favored ten. His short ministry was one continued scene
of most blessed outpourings of the Holy Spirit. He was
eminently the revivalist of this apostolic company. One of
the most highly blessed fields of his preaching was in the
region of the Schuylkill river, some twenty-five miles from
Philadelphia. Among those who were savingly interested
in that blessed work of grace were the grandfather and
grandmother of REV. ARCHIBALD ALEXANDER. It was
eminently a memorable day in our Zion, and a happy day
for our land, when the covenant of the Lord was ratified in
that family. DR. ARCHIBALD ALEXANDER, what endless
streams of sacred influence was he the instrument of opening! Placed at the head of Princeton Seminary, when it
was first opened for the training of young men for the
gospel ministry, and continued therein for nearly forty
years, who can estimate the grandeur of the work to which
he was called! Nearly forty years, forty classes, one every
year leaving that school of the prophets—thousands in all,
many of whom have been among the most godly and successful ministers of our whole Church! Then when we

consider the spirit which he infused into these young men—
his own spirit of simple piety, earnest godliness, sound and
sanctified common-sense, how can we sufficiently admire
that wonderful stream of influence?

" Take as a sample of what it was, the single class, a body
of whose surviving members are here to-day to sympathize
and rejoice with our Brother NILES, who was one of our
number. Here is Brother CRAWFORD, spared for forty
years, and permitted to work on with faithfulness and hope
and love as God gave him strength in this region of the
great vineyard. Here is Brother ERSKINE, a theological
standard-bearer of our Church, the able editor for years of
one of the most influential journals of our beloved Presbyterianism, and the pastor who is himself a power for truth
and Christ. Here is Brother PAXTON, who has nobly stood
in the high places of our Zion, as pastor of churches which
exerted the widest influence in the whole general assembly,
and now as professor in the seminary, where we all once
sat at the feet of the sainted ALEXANDER, and MILLER of
whom he is the honored successor. Here is our beloved
Brother NILES, the five and twentieth anniversary of whose
pastorate in this church we are joining to celebrate. How
well God has enabled him to do his work here, we have
heard with wonder and joy. How much he is beloved by
this dear people we see in the outgushing of affection which
is manifested by every method by which it could be made
known.

" And here is our beloved and honored Brother CATTELL
also with us in these delightful ceremonies. Though not a
member of the same class with us, he was so near that we
may adopt him, at least for this occasion. To say nothing
of the work he first did as pastor of one of our most influential churches, and of the work he is now doing as secre-

tary of the Board of Ministerial Relief, who shall describe
his grand work, for many years as the president of La
Fayette College. On how many young men did he exert
an influence that will tell evermore.

"And so we might speak of forty classes which up to our
day had left that school of the prophets on whom DR.
ALEXANDER had left his impress. And again since that
day, forty other classes have gone forth from the same
centre, to exert their beneficent power on the world.

"Thus may we trace that single line of godly influence
which may well be termed hereditary.

"Fully two centuries and an half ago we trace its spring
in DR. KENNEDY, an eminently godly minister of Ulster,
Ireland,—then in his daughter CATHARINE, wife of the
founder of the Log College,—then in the blessed ten evangelists of that honored institution,—then in the great
revival under ROWLAND,—then in the conversion of the
ancestors of DR. ALEXANDER,—then in the peerless piety
and wisdom of that blessed man,—then in the glorious
history of Princeton Seminary,—and then in the thousands
who with ourselves have gone out from that God-honored
institution. Is not all this wonderful, wonderful, wonderful! Is not the hand of God seen moving every spring, and
directing every movement! Is He not true, gloriously
true to His everlasting covenant!"

Following DR. MURPHY, DR. PAXTON spoke with great
impressiveness upon the subject assigned for the evening:
The pastoral office, as appointed by God, in its various
relations to the Church and to society. "A pastorate such
as we celebrate now," he said, "who shall estimate its full
significance. It points to

"Twenty-five years of Bible study.

"Twenty-five years of prayer and walking with God.
"Twenty-five years of sympathy with the sorrowing.
"Twenty-five years of watching over the young and tempted.
"Twenty-five years of faithful pulpit service.
"Twenty-five years, an example and a guide for others in the way to Heaven.

"What a comment on the character of a pastor and on the love and devotion of a people, does such a history present!"
After singing "Let Zion's Watchmen all Awake" DR. ROBINSON followed in a brief address, speaking of his former associations with DR. NILES, when they were neighboring pastors, and of the pleasant memories which came to his mind on this glad occasion.

DR. CATTELL was the last speaker, who, after referring to the endowments of mind and heart neccessary alike in minister and people in order to secure long and happy pastorates, said somewhat as follows:

"We are all indebted to DR. MURPHY for the interesting facts he stated with reference to CATHARINE KENNEDY. I must admit that I never before heard of this good woman; but now that I have learned of the part she took, nearly two centuries ago, in forming the character of our dear DR. NILES, I shall ever cherish for her a deep sense of personal gratitude. For, like all these brethren who have spoken, I have long known and loved the Doctor; and he has been so helpful to me in the Board of Ministerial Relief (of which he has long been a member) that I often wonder how, as the executive officer of the Board, I could have got along without him. All the kind things, therefore, that his classmates and DR. ROBINSON have said about my honored and beloved friend, I wish not only to adopt as my own senti-

ments, but 1 want to say them over again in italics! And
I could even add a good deal more! Yes, CATHARINE
KENNEDY 'builded better than she knew' for me and for
the Board of Relief and for the Presbyterian Church and for
this congregation, when she started the influences that gave
us DR. NILES.

"But I more than suspect I know somebody who has had
more to do than CATHARINE had in forming his character
and in thus fitting him for the great work he has accomplished for you and for us all. Every man is pretty much
what his wife makes him. This is specially true of a
minister. About ninety-nine hundredths of whatever good
a pastor does may be set down to the credit of a blessed
woman in the manse! I happen to know something of the
strong, but tender and gentle influence that has pervaded
yonder manse and made it one of the sweetest homes on
earth. I must not dwell upon this—but well do I know
that my brother's thoughts, during all the congratulations
of this happy anniversary, have constantly and with a
tender and manly love turned toward the wife who, during
all these twenty-five years of his labor in your midst, has
stood by his side.

"But though I may not dwell upon what she has been to
her husband—nor to her children, who have grown to be
manly men and who requite her love and care with filial
devotion—I must remind you of what, as your pastor's
wife, she has been to you and to your children. Her name
was not mentioned in the Call you sent to her husband a
quarter of a century ago, but you know what she has done
in the parish work all these years. You know with what
untiring energy, with what exhaustless love, with what
refined delicacy and tact she has sought out ways of help-
fulness among you, so that your hearts have been knit to

hers. It is natural that her husband should be the central
figure in the grateful rejoicings of this anniversary—she
herself would have it so. But we cannot look at him and
not think of her : and the prayer of us all to the great
Head of the Church is that for yet many, many years her
presence, as well as that of her husband, may enrich your
lives."

The choir then sang a beautiful Easter anthem. Prayer
was offered by REV. GEORGE L. SMITH of the Calvary
Presbyterian Church, and the Benediction was pronounced
by DR. NILES, after which many of the people crowded
around the pulpit to shake their pastor's hand and to rejoice
with him over the most delightful and memorable service
ever known in the history of the church.

The following from an editorial which appeared next
(Monday) morning in the *York Gazette*, may properly be
inserted here.

"The exercises in the First Presbyterian Church yesterday, commemorative of the twenty-fifth anniversary of the
pastorate of DR. NILES were most appropriate and well-
calculated profoundly to impress both pastor and people.

"Evidently, this church, during the period under review,
has been most prosperous, and that, too, in the very best
sense. It has not only sent off two additional churches
from its bosom, but it has also, as shown by the following
figures, contributed an amount of money in aid of the different departments of church work, truly Christian in
character, that is perfectly astounding.

"The figures are as follows :

"Expenses for Home Purposes.   .   .   : $130,000
      "   "   General Assembly.   .   .   .   791

"	"	Foreign Missions.	. .	22,950
"	"	Home Missions.	. . .	26,642
"	"	Education.	. . .	5,659
"	"	Publication.	. . .	3,156
"	"	Sunday-school Work.	.	6,102
"	"	Church Erection.	.	4,797
"	"	Ministeral Relief.	. . .	11,027
"	"	Freedmen and Lincoln University		10,599
"	"	Sustentation.	. . .	3,007
"	"	Aid for Colleges.	. .	456
"	"	Other charities.	. . .	13,774

Total. $238,960

"When we consider for what this large sum was contributed, we must conclude that the giving of much of it was prompted by a truly Christian spirit.

"Surely, the review, as presented yesterday, of DR. NILES' pastorate at the First Presbyterian Church, must be a source of very great comfort and encouragement both to that gentleman and to his very estimable lady, who seems especially endowed with those rare qualities of head and heart, so necessary for the successful discharge of the arduous and delicate duties devolving upon a pastor's wife.

"Briefly, it would seem both pastor and people have been especially fortunate in the relation they have sustained to each other; and, with the earnest hope that the health and strength of the former may be graciously vouchsafed him for many years to come, this flourishing church should continue its Christian work with unabated zeal."

CONGREGATIONAL RECEPTION.
TUESDAY EVENING, APRIL 8.

AT seven o'clock, the church was crowded by members and friends of the congregation, together with the Presbytery of Westminster (which had adjourned its meeting at Wrightsville, to be present on this occasion) and ministers of different denominations in the city, and other personal friends of the pastor. The superb decorations of Sunday remained, and with the addition of fresh flowers, gave the church even more of a festival appearance than on that day. After an organ voluntary, the choir rendered in exquisite style, Wilkinson's "Festival Cantate Domino," which was followed by a Prayer of Invocation by the moderator of Presbytery, PROF. SAMUEL A. MARTIN, of Lincoln University.

DR. McDOUGALL, president of the York Collegiate Institute, as chairman of the meeting, in a felicitous opening address, welcomed the audience in behalf of the committee of arrangements, and introduced the speakers for the evening.

After another beautiful selection by the choir, MR. HENRY SMALL, chairman of the committee on invitations, announced a variety of acknowledgments and congratulatory messages received by post and telegraph. Among these was one from REV. DR. SUNDERLAND of Washington, D. C., which conveyed assurances of his deep interest in the celebration, and said: "From personal observation, I can testify to the true and loyal affection of your people for their pastor. And I congratulate him on being able to hold his position so long, on one of the most prominent watchtowers of our American Zion. Long may this relation of pastor and people endure. And may God shower IIis blessings upon you all."

Other communications were from REV. DR. R. M. PATTERSON of Philadelphia, eloquent with congratulations and good wishes;

DR. E. T. JEFFERS, professor in Lincoln University;

HON. JUDGE FURST of Bellefonte;

REV. N. G. PARKE, D. D., of Pittston;

REV. E. S. MAPES of Carlisle, for himself and his people of the First Presbyterian Church;

GEN. JAMES A. BEAVER, Governor of Pennsylvania, regretting his inability to attend, and wishing that the future years may be even yet more fruitful of good results from the happy union.

A letter was also received from the moderator of the General Assembly, REV. W. C. ROBERTS, D.D., L.L. D., of Lake Forest University, Chicago, in which he says: "Not often is a congregation blessed with such a pastor, and from personal knowledge, I can add, it is not very often that a good pastor has such a people. It is a happy occasion all around. May the union continue many years to come. Enter together into new experiences and new fields for doing good."

II. C. NILES, ESQ., was next called for, who made announcement of letters addressed directly to the pastor, among which were:

1st. An affectionate and beautiful communication from

Rev. Dr. Gotwald, of Springfield, Ohio, formerly pastor
of St. Paul's Church, York; in which he reviews their 16
years' acquaintance, and particularly the period when side
by side, in this city, they labored with utmost harmony and
fraternal coöperation. " As I recall these delightful memories," he says, "and think of all that you have been to me,
instinctively, from the very depth of my heart I say: God
bless you my dear, constant true, brother and friend."

2nd. From Rev. Dr. Nelson of Philadelphia, for a little
while before the war, co-presbyter with Dr. Niles in St.
Louis, recalling the anxieties and labors of those ante bellum
days, and congratulating him on the peaceful, happy, fruitful
quarter century God has since given him in York.

3d. From Rev. Dr. J. J. Porter of Phelps, N. Y., a
friend from college and seminary days, and also a neighboring pastor in St. Louis at the time the war broke out.

4th. From Rev. Joseph K. Wight, a classmate at Princeton Seminary, now in Florida, and

5th. A similar one from Rev. Dr. J. Addison Henry,
of West Philadelphia., who says: "I have profound
respect for the man who preaches in one pulpit for a quarter
of a century: but outside of that, I have an affection for
you, my dear brother, which but for special engagements on
April 6th, would draw me to the scene of your rejoicing."

6th. From Rev. Dr. Matthews of London, England,
traveling companion with our pastor some years ago in
Europe. Had he carried out his original plan to leave
Liverpool for New York March 19th, he could easily have
been here to share in the gladness of this occasion. He
adds: "We have here a dignitary of the Episcopal
Church, who calls himself 'Ebor' because he is Archbishop of York. What peculiar title should be given to

you, whom we may call the Patriarch of York? In England an archbishop is styled 'His Grace,' but in the Orient
is spoken of as 'His Beatitude.' So, my brother, we have
found how to speak of *you,* to whom the lines have fallen
in pleasant places!"

7th. Next from REV. DR. CUYLER of Brooklyn, who
exclaims: "All Hail! my beloved Brother NILES! I
reach out my hand to you in sincere congratulations. You
have had 25 years of hard, honest, Heaven-blessed work.
The sheaves have been garnered, and the harvester has a
right to rejoice and be thankful. By a singular coincidence,
I am to close my thirty years' delightful pastorate in this
noble church, on the very same morning when you will be
celebrating your 'silver nuptials.' Well, we have both
had a happy career under the old blue Presbyterian flag,
and will have some things to talk about when we get home
to 'our Father's House'! God bless you on and on and
evermore, until the glory breaks!"

8th. Next, one in happy pleasantry from REV. M. D.
BABCOCK of Baltimore. After congratulations to pastor
and people, he says: "I will not express my amazement
that you could stand each other so long! There is food
for wonder in it all the same! With so much restlessness
in human nature, your mutual record is splendid. Leibnitz's
doctrine of 'Pre-established Harmony' is far from out-
lawed! God bless you, and increase your power to bless.
And may God bless your wife, who has kept you in hand
so long and saved you from so many mistakes. Perhaps
the quintessence of congratulation would be: 'To the
woman, who blessed the *man,* who blessed the *church,*
which blessed the *town* of York!'"

9th. Other notes of congratulation were announced as

from: Revs. G. W. Enders, II. II. Weber, A. G. Fastnacht,
A. M. Barnitz, and B. C. Conner, of this city; Messrs. J. H.
Sternberg of Reading, F. L. Danforth of Buffalo, Hon.
Alfred Lockhart of Washington, W. II. H. Moore, Esq., of
New York, M. C. Parker of St. Louis, John P. Ammidon
of Baltimore, Rev. John Paul Egbert of Buffalo, N. Y.,
Rev. J. L. Jenkins D.D., of Pittsfield, Mass., Rev. Dr.
Prime, one of the editors of the *New York Observer*, Rev.
Dr. Robbins of Philadelphia, Rev. D. Bingham of Oxford,
Rev. Dr. Stryker of New York, Rev. R. P. Cobb of Mer-
chantville, N. J., Rev. Prof. Jones of Lincoln University,
Rev. T. Ralston Smith D.D., of Buffalo, N. Y., Rev. Dr.
Joseph T. Smith of Baltimore, Rev. Dr. F. W. Conrad,
editor of the *Lutheran Observer*, Rev. W. L. Ledwith of
Philadelphia, Rev. Geo. B. Stewart of Harrisburg, and from
Rev. Henry Darling D.D., LL.D., President of Hamilton
College, who preached the sermon when DR. NILES was
ordained to the gospel ministry, by the Presbytery of
Columbia.

From the twin brothers, REV. D. McCLELLAN BUTT and
REV. SCOTT BUTT, who were brought up and educated in
this church and are now laboring as home missionaries in
South Dakota. One of them writes: "I want to congratulate you upon your long and successful pastorate; and also
add my appreciation of, and interest in, your noble work.
You see I still call you "*Pastor*," and it comes naturally,
for I have known no other. To brother and myself you
have been a spiritual father, and the influence you exerted
over my life you little imagine. From my earliest recollection you have been to me an example and a counselor.
Your thoughts and words have been a great help to me
here on the frontier, and as I remember them they are
sources of joy." The other in a similar strain says: "I

can not thank you enough for your spiritual training and pastoral interest, and you shall always be held in loving remembrance."

REV. DR. KENDALL of New York, senior secretary of the Board of Home Missions, says: "It would have given me great pleasure to have attended the 25th anniversary of your installation at York, if I could have found it possible to go. I hope your Historical Review will be published and an account of the other proceedings and that I may be remembered in the list of those that receive it. God bless you my dear brother, and prolong your days and your usefulness, is the prayer of

"Yours very truly,

"H. KENDALL."

After these announcements, five minute addresses were called for by the chairman, and the first to respond was REV. THOMAS M. CRAWFORD, who spoke in substance, as follows: "While there are those present, as our esteemed friend DR. HECKMAN, who were classmates of DR. NILES, and others who stand in the relation of co-presbyters, I am doubly related, being both classmate and co-presbyter. My thoughts very naturally carry me back over the years, to Princeton Theological Seminary, where for the first time we met as fellow-students. Soon it became apparent that our brother was an earnest, diligent, and successful student, possessed of a spirit of earnest and consistent piety, and intellectually above the average of his class.

"We always anticipated for DR. NILES a prominent position in the Church. This anticipation has been realized. The expected position has been reached and is now recognized by all who know him.

"These beautiful and brilliant surroundings, which so

please our eyes, and charm our ears, and enliven our spirits, have a deep significance. They tell the story of twenty-five years of unremitting labor, of earnest prayer, of thorough organization, of careful thought, of incessant effort, of close study and of requited toil.

"As a co-presbyter of DR. NILES, I desire to bear testimony to the salutary influence exerted by himself and this church of York upon our Presbytery and its churches. DR. NILES is not only the pastor, faithful and beloved, of the First Church of York, but has also proved himself to be a friend of all our churches, by his active interest in, care for, and oversight of all of them. In conclusion, we heartily congratulate DR. NILES upon this auspicious day, and the church and people of York for so nobly coming up to the more than ordinary requirements of this grand occasion."

REV. DR. C. W. STEWART next spoke as representative of the Presbytery, referring to the happy fraternal relations which have always existed between its member and especially to the high position and influence maintained by the pastor and church at York.

SALUTATIONS FROM NEIGHBORING CHURCHES.

M. B. F. WILLIS, one of the ruling elders in the Calvary Presbyterian Church, was next introduced, and spoke in substance, as follows:

"*Mr. Chairman:*—I feel that I cannot add much of interest to what has been so well said by those who have preceded me, to-night. I am here, however, to speak for Calvary Church, so happily referred to by yourself as one of the 'two vigorous daughters'—a numbers of whose members join with you in this evening service. I feel that some personal explanation is due those in this large audience who may not know your speaker—for it was not my privilege to have been born into this fold.

"Thirteen years ago this coming month of June, came to the beautiful and historic town of York—was one of those to whom you, DR. NILES, referred in your interesting and graphic historical address of last Sunday morning, as having been 'welcomed from sister' churches. In the fall of '83 a handful of us went out from your midst to form what is now known as the York Calvary Presbyterian Church. So few indeed were we in number, that it could almost have been said of us what ARTEMUS WARD said of his company of one hundred men raised during the war of the rebellion (for different reasons, however, he out of courtesy, we out of sheer necessity) that 'they were all officers.' Some of us indeed, were obliged to hold two and even more offices at one and the same time. All is now changed—to-day we number on our rolls one hundred and eighty odd members. Doctor in your historical review you said that when we went out we were 'sadly missed.' We are not sorry to know that we were thus well thought of. But if our absence from among you was felt, how must it have fared with us? I think we all felt about as I did when, at the age of eight years, our father purchased a farm that was henceforth to be our home—and took us far away from our native village. I have a vivid recollection of how when the night drew on and the big teams and their drivers that had brought us started on their return journey, I cried to go back to the dear old home. Perhaps we are not quite ready to own to the tears for what we gave up in going out from you to begin the new home, but we can assure you, sir, there was and is a warm place in our affections for this place and its associations of hallowed memories, and now—while the cares and responsi-

bilities of a numerous and growing church family press
upon us—we still find time on occasions of this kind, to
gladly return and rejoice with you. As Virginia has been
called the Mother of Presidents so may not you and this
people be fitly called 'the mother of churches' in this
growing city of York! In conclusion, Doctor, if we were
missed for number and usefulness, surely it is no longer so,
for at every return, we see faces of new sons and daughters
here in ever-increasing numbers, and to-day your church
family seems larger than ever before and so may it ever
be!"

Following Mr. Willis, Prof. A. B. Carner, elder in
the Westminster Church, spoke as follows:

"*Mr. Chairman, Ladies and Gentlemen, Friends:*—On such
an occasion and in such a gathering as this, any man might
be proud to have a part. The one who ought to have this
honor in my place is my 'true yoke-fellow,' Mr. Harry
Myers, who by his long experience in our field is best
acquainted with it.

" Westminster, the younger of the two daughters of this
venerable and honored church, sends you greeting. We
are scarcely three years old, and not yet very sturdy, but
we have great perservance, great hope and faith, and we
are striving to teach the good word that some of us have
been so well taught by you. We bring to the mother-
church our dutiful and affectionate salutations, our congratulations, and our good wishes for all the years to come.

" Now the Lord of peace himself give you peace always
by all means."

Rev. W. S. Freas, pastor of St. Paul's Lutheran Church
of this city, next spoke in a felicitious manner, in behalf of
the various denominations of Christian people in York, and
read the following paper, unanimously adopted at a meeting

of the Pastoral Association held on Monday, April 7, 1890 :

" WHERAS, The First Presbyterian Church of this city is now celebrating the *Quarto Centennial* of the pastorate of REV. II. E. NILES, D. D.. and,

" WHEREAS, That congregation has always been among the foremost to further the efforts inaugurated by this association for the promotion of order and religion in this community, and its honored pastor, DR. NILES, has been one of our most regular and efficient members, therefore

" *Resolved*, That this Association congratulate the First Presbyterian Church of this city on the auspicious circumstances under which it celebrates this anniversary ; that we record our recognition of the marked degree of success that has characterized the ministry of DR. NILES in our midst, and our high appreciation of those qualities of heart and mind which have won, and retained for so long a period, the esteem and appreciation of so intelligent and prominent a congregation, and that we hereby express our prayers that he may be spared yet many years, to his church and to us.

" *Resolved*, That we accept the invitation to be present during the anniversary exercise now being held, and that we appoint REV. W. S. FREAS to represent our association and bear to the First Presbyterian Church and its pastor an expresssion of our sentiments.

" A. G. FASTNACHT,
" Secretary Pastoral Association,
" York, Pa."

At this stage in the proceedings, an event took place which, though not indicated in the programme, proved to be of great interest to all concerned.

MR. JOHN HAMILTON SMALL, stepping forward before

the congregation, began to address the pastor in well-chosen
words of affectionate regard, and in the name of the
people to offer some tangible evidence of their grateful
appreciation.

As he spoke he unfolded a beautiful white star which he
intimated might be symbolic of the clean white pages of
history, twenty-five years ago, that we look back upon
to-day and of that final reward which is assured to a faithful minister who turns many to righteousness.

Then at length removing the white paper covering, he
showed that star-shaped figure formed of *twenty-five gold
double eagles* ingeniousiy arranged—the star now changed
to gold! as are those pages of history of twenty-five years
golden with the records of a faithful pastorate and a devoted
people. This the pastor was asked to accept from those
to whom he had ministered in their varied experiences of
joy or sorrow.

DR. NILES, scarcely able to command his emotions,
replied in substance :—That this event though not prean-
nounced, could hardly be called a surprise. Many things
not definitely expected, when they occur, seem almost a
matter of course. *E. y.* A short time ago when he looked
out on the lawn of the churchyard, which had laid brown
and bare in the rigors of winter, he was not surprised that
it had suddenly changed to verdure and brightness, because
he knew that warm suns had begun to shine and April
showers to fall. Neither was he surprised when the
feathered troupe which had been travelling and giving con-
certs in the south, came back to fill our atmosphere with the
music of bird songs, because such is their instinctive custom
in this glad opening season. In like manner, it was not
wonderful, when a people, who for many years, have been
caring for the temporal wants of their spiritual leader,

take another opportunity to manifest their thoughtful devotion. Loyal, loving, generous hearts are always prompting to timely and generous deeds. And now, on this public occasion, he was glad to bear testimony to the uniform kindness and liberality with which he and his family have been treated. Neither could he fail to appreciate the beautiful and touching address of his young brother, who had not only expressed the kind regards of the congregation, but also by the manner in which he performed that office, and even by the tones of his voice, had so vividly brought to mind the person of his sainted father, who, when he was with us, was so eloquent of speech, and so ready for deeds of generous affection.

To all who had taken part in the preparation and conduct of this quarto-centennial anniversary, DR. NILES extended assurances of his grateful appreciation. Also to his brethren of the Presbytery, who had suspended their regular session that they might come hither to take part in these festivities. Also to the clergy of York who were present in goodly number and whose sentiments of fraternal regard had been so nobly voiced by the brother whom they had appointed. And to the Christian people of the city—known by different denominational distinctions, who had manifested so much interest in our joy, and who, in the different services had been present with us, illustrating by their lively sympathies what all formally acknowledge " We believe in the communion of saints."

The last address was by REV. GEO. C. HECKMAN, D. D., of Reading, who spoke somewhat as follows:

" Humorous allusions have been made to the disclosures which such anniversaries make of the age of classmates. Well! a useful old age is an honor from God. All that this anniversary proves is, that DR. NILES and his classmates

participating in these delightful exercises have been in the
ministry twenty-five years, and that in DR. NILES' case that
these have been twenty-five years of memorable usefulness.
But the roll of a class is no better indication of the relative
age of its members than the roll of a Presbytery is of the
age of its members, where the early ordination of a
minister may put below him a long list of members older
than he, sometimes one old enough to be his father. Thus
in our class at Princeton the average was very much above
the age of the younger members. DR. NILES and I were in
a class which through the course of three years enrolled
some sixty-seven members, about one half of whom are
still living. One of our classmates had a daughter fifteen
years old. The brother next above me on the roll was ten
years my senior, and the one next below me graduated at
Jefferson College four years before I was born. There was
Brother ——, about twenty-five years my senior, I suppose,
for his natal day is modestly withheld from the records of
the seminary. On parting I asked: ' Brother ———,
where do you expect to settle.' ' Well,' answered he,
' I don't intend to be in a hurry. I think I will spend
eight or ten years east of the Alleghenies, and then finally
settle somewhere in the west.' So you see what a hopeful
set we were. Of course these were exceptional cases, and I
only introduce them to challenge the misapprehension
that might arise from the remarks of the dear gray-haired
brother, who, in his admirable speech, indicated a fear that
his nativity might be put too far forward, as a classmate
of DR. NILES.

" I came here to-night under the expectation that I had
but a minute or two for salutations and congratulations.
Now I learn that it is the desire that I should speak without any limitation of time. Well, I am deeply sensible of

the honor, but I am not prepared to do justice to the unex-
pected privilege. You have already heard enough to
exhaust an ordinary audience. But as this is not an ordinary
occasion so it is not an ordinary audience. It is really
wonderful after the several crowded services that have
fitly commemorated this historic anniversary, here is
another crowded house, that has listened to any number of
letters, speeches and anthems, all admirably rendered, without sign of exhaustion or alarm, even of a speaker who is
announced to speak *ad libitum*, which in Latin for ' As long
as you please.'

"In my youth, say a few years ago, I heard a story
which I shall remember when I am an old man, which has
done me (and my audiences) a world of good for many years.
There was a men who attended the prayer-meeting with
commendable punctuality. Some of you know him from
painful experience. He was an awful bore, and I use that
young ladies' commonplace epithet with etymological
exactness. One evening Brother Bore sat half through the
meeting without breaking silence, itself an ominous
phenomenon not without disturbing influence in the
spiritual atmosphere. Then he sprang to his feet, exclaim-
ing, ' Brethren I have just had a severe struggle with the
devil. He has been telling me that I am a burden to the
prayer-meeting; that I weary without edifying you; that
I had better be still, and that you would all like it better
if I was: but, brethren, I have gained the victory over the
devil, and I am going to speak.' And he did with the
usual demoralizing effect, destroying the remaining half
hour of the meeting. After the benediction the pastor
passed quickly to the brother, and laying his hand on his
shoulder, whispered, ' Brother Bore, I believe the devil was
right.' Well, I have always kept the courageous humor

of that pastor in mind, and I will now, and not abuse the privilege so courteously accorded me to-night.

"It was a sore disappointment not to be with my class-mates here last Sabbath. My western residence has made our meeting rare, and death has made others impossible. Near the centre of the roll of our class is a block of fifteen names, between those of DR. ERSKINE and BISHOP LITTLEJOHN, in the midst of which my name alone stands without the star of death, the sole survivor of the fifteen. In the centre of our class, death has been especially busy, beginning its work in the seminary. Thus out from among the dead my name looks in longing for my surviving comrades. For none of them have I ever held a warmer heart and higher respect than for your beloved pastor, so widely known and highly esteemed wherever known. This has been the growth of sentiment felt on our first acquaintance in the seminary. When I conducted our class prayer-meeting, your pastor was always asked to take part, as one whose voice we always liked to hear. That youthful estimate I can and do regard with modest com-placency, for God has confirmed it by honor, usefulness and happiness with which He has crowned the long and faith-ful ministry of your dear pastor. With the unanimous verdict of this crowded assembly, do I endorse heartily the truthful expression of praise well earned, which this faith-ful ministry and Christian character have received in the numerous letters and addresses to which you have listened with eagerness and delight during these commemorative ceremonies."

After another selection by the choir, the entire congrega-tion arose and sang :

> " Blest be the tie that binds
> Our hearts in Christian Love."

The people were then invited to pass in companies of about three hundred into the chapel, where DR. NILES and his wife were requested to take their stand and receive the personal salutations of their friends . After the handshaking which was so long continued and hearty, that many began to fear it might exhaust the smiling pair who made the centre of the brilliant scene, the guests passed up to the spacious Sunday-school room which had been converted into a banquet-hall, tastefully decorated with palms and tropical plants and flowers, while the tables, loaded with luscious trophies of the gastronomic art, were gracefully served by fair women and maidens who seemed anxious to promote the greatest happiness of all. Those waiting their turn in the church, were in the meantime regaled by the choir, with five musical selections, and not until a late hour were the last guests waited on, and the last words of congratulation uttered. From beginning to end the celebration had been AN ENTIRE SUCCESS.

HISTORICAL SKETCH.

THE beginnings of what was originally known as "The Religious Society of English Presbyterians in and near the town of York," are involved in much obscurity. As far back as 1762 it appears that a little company of such as preferred the doctrines and order of Presbyterianism were ministered unto more or less regularly, by supplies furnished by the Presbytery of Donegal, whose territory included the counties of Chester and Lancaster, and all west of them. Subsequently, such supplies were mostly connected with the Presbytery of Carlisle, until the year 1793, when the congregation at York united with that of Round Hill, in Hopewell township, in extending a call to the REV. ROBERT CATHCART, who had recently emigrated from the county of Londonderry, north of Ireland, and had united with the Presbytery of Philadelphia. [MR. CATHCART had studied at the college in Glasgow, Scotland, and after licensure by the Presbytery of Route, had preached within its bounds, for several years, before coming to this country. Afterwards, in 1816, he received the honorary title of Doctor of Divinity from the Queen's,—now Rutgers College of New Jersey.] The call was accepted, and after ordination by the Presbytery of Carlisle, DR. CATHCART became pastor of the two congregations about twenty miles apart, preaching to them on alternate Sabbaths, visiting their families yearly and catechising both young and old. At the time of his settlement, this congregation seems to have contained about twenty-five families, and only six communicants, all of whom were females. It is a matter of regret that the names of those who signed the call for this first pastor cannot now be given. But among them we are sure were those of JOHN FORSYTH, who went to Philadelphia and made arrangements for the introduction of DR. CATHCART to this people; of JAMES SMITH, one of the signers of the Declaration of Independence, whose remains sleep in our churchyard: of GEORGE IRWIN, of DOCTOR WILLIAM KENNEDY, of WILLIAM McCLELLAN and of JENNET GRIER. For about twenty years, (until 1812 or 1813,) the affairs of this small congregation seem to have been managed without special regard to established forms. No regular meetings were held for attention to secular matters, and owing to the lack of male communicants, there were for several years no elders to care for the spiritual interests. Yet all things moved on harmoniously, a few active individuals co-operating with the pastor, whose regularity, punctuality and good judgment were abundant guaranty to all. At length, however, when it was deemed necessary to place the financial affairs on a permanent basis, application was made to the authorities of the Commonwealth for a charter of incorporation. It was granted to the REV. ROBERT CATHCART, WM. HARRIS, JOHN FORSYTH, JOHN GRIER, WM. BARBER, JAMES JOHNSON and PENROSE ROBINSON, and their successors duly elected, "to have continuance forever thereafter, by the name, style and title of THE TRUSTEES OF THE ENGLISH PRESBYTERIAN CONGREGATION IN THE BOROUGH OF YORK."

This charter, being duly certified by SIMON SNYDER, Governor, and recorded in the office of NATHANIEL B.

BOILEAU, Secretary of the Commonwealth, December 9, 1813, took effect from that date.

The first annual election under the charter, was on the first Monday in May, 1814, at which time the following trustees were elected, viz: REV. ROBERT CATHCART, WM. BARBER, ESQ., JAMES JOHNSON, PENROSE ROBINSON, JAMES KELLY ESQ., and JOHN IRWIN. A few years after, on the list of trustees appear the names of DAVID CASSATT, ESQ., and DR. WILLIAM MCILVAINE, and a little later, those of DAVID B. PRINCE and PHILIP A. SMALL.

Since that time, the following have served for various periods, or are now (1890) serving as members of this Board: Jacob Emmit, Thomas C. Hambly, Jonathan McMurdy, Thomas Kelly, Henry M. McClellan, Samuel Small, E. M. Donaldson, John Evans, William R. Morris, James B. Latimer, Peter Emmit, David G. Barnitz, Edward Chapin, Robert C. Woodward, James W. Kerr, Eli Lewis, Henry Welsh, Erastus H. Weiser, Samuel S. Hersh, Emerson J. Case, David E. Small, Samuel Small Jr., John J. Reed, John H. Small, George H. Billmeyer, Henry Small, Wm. H. McClellan, Wm. H. Griffith, and James McLean.

The lot of ground which from the beginning has been held by this congregation was granted by JOHN PENN Senior, and JOHN PENN, Junior, heirs of WILLIAM PENN, and proprietaries of the state of Pennsylvania, to GEORGE IRWIN, WM. SCOTT and ARCHIBALD McLEAN in trust, in the year 1785. Between this time and the installation of DR. CATHCART, probably about 1790, the first house of worship was erected. It was a plain brick building, to which various improvements were subsequently added from time to time, according to the increasing necessities of the people. The most thorough and important of these changes were previous to the meeting in this place of the Synod of Pennsyl-

vania, memorable because of the trial of REV. ALBERT
BARNES for alleged heresy in doctrine, which was one of
the steps that led to the disruption of the Presbyterian
church in 1837. The congregation continued to worship
in this sanctuary until 1860, when it was taken down to
give place for the present commodious and beautiful
edifice. In June of that year, the corner stone was laid
with appropriate religious ceremonies, the pastor, REV.
THOMAS STREET, being assisted therein by REV. DR. DE-
WITT of Harrisburg, and REV. DR. E. E. ADAMS of Philadelphia. During the pastorate of DR. CATHCART (about
1814) a brick parsonage was erected on the grounds of the
society, which with various modifications continued the
home of successive pastors, until March, 1886, when it
was removed and foundations laid for the present con-
venient, healthful and tasteful manse which was finished in
April of the following year.

The present two-story chapel, so important a part of our
church property, was erected in 1867 in place of a small
frame building which had previously been used for social
meetings and for Sunday-school purposes.

Near the close of DR. CATHCART'S pastorate, the first regular church session seems to have existed, the ruling elders
being DR. WILLIAM McILVAINE, who was ordained July 19,
1835, and continued in office until the date of his death;
and PETER McINTYRE, who served in the office about two
years. Subsequently the following have been appointed to
this office, viz:

H. M. McClellan, M. D.,	Ordained Jan.	6, 1839,	Died Aug. 7, 1869.
Jacob Emmit,	" July	5, 1840,	" July 2, 1865.
Samuel Small,	"	1850,	" July 14, 1885.
James W. Kerr, M. D.,	" Oct.	14, 1855,	" June 10, 1889.
David Etter Small,	" April	16, 1865,	" March 25, 1883.

John M. Brown,	"	Feb.	1870,		
Erastus H. Weiser,	"	Feb.	1870,	" July 11,	1872.
Samuel Small, Jr.,	"	May 30, 1877, Resigned March 31, 1886.			
Joseph Root,	"	May 30, 1877,			
Wm. Henry McClellan,	"	Dec.	2, 1887,		
Henry Small,	"	Dec.	2, 1887,		

The following have also served as deacons in this church :

Jacob H. Huber,	Ordained 1870.		Died	1876.
Charles G. Welsh,	"	"	Dismissed	1874.
James C. Luitweiler,	"	"	"	1883.
Henry S. Myers,	"	"	"	1887.
Niles H. Shearer, M. D.,	"	"		
Isaac A. Elliott,	"	1877.		
Wm H. McClellan,	"	"		

After a service of 42 years in the united congregations of York and Hopewell, in the year 1835, DR. CATHCART resigned his charge of the latter, and in accordance with the general desire of the people in York, devoted all his attention to this field.

But after two more years, in 1837, the infirmities of age began so to tell upon his robust constitution, that he also relinquished this pastorate. Thenceforth, to the end of his days, he continued a regular attendant upon the services of the church, and in the quiet home circle surrounded by children and grandchildren, passed the evening of life, until at the age of 90, on the 19th of Oct., 1849, he was called up to the Heavenly Rest.

His successor in the pastoral office was REV. BENJAMIN J. WALLACE, D. D., who was installed on the 9th of May, 1839, and continued here until September, 1845, when he was dismissed to accept a professorship in Delaware College. Afterwards he resided in Pittsburg, and from thence removed to Philadelphia, where he became editor of the "Presbyterian Quarterly Review," and so continued until his death, July 25, 1862.

Rev. Daniel Hopkins Emerson, D.D., a native of Salem, Mass., member of the Third Presbytery of Philadelphia, was next called to this pastorate, October 1st, 1845, and continued in it till April, 1855, when he was dismissed to engage in the work of the American and Foreign Christian Union. Soon, however, he returned to the pastoral office at St. George's, Delaware, where he remained until 1868. Subsequently in Oswego, N. Y., as secretary of the Y. M. C. A., and in Philadelphia, as pastor of the Eastburn Mariner's Church, and missionary for the First Presbyterian Church, he was eminently useful and beloved, until his death, July 6, 1883.

Rev. Charles J. Hutchins, a licentiate of the Presbytery of Erie, was invited to supply the pulpit in June, 1855, and in October of the same year, was ordained and installed pastor.

Here he wrought earnestly and efficiently until April, 1859, the four years of his pastorate constituting a period of spiritual activity and of increase in numbers and power to the church.

Soon after leaving York, he became a pastor at Racine, Wisconsin, from whence he entered the army as chaplain of the 39th Regiment of that State, and was noted for his courage and enthusiasm.

After the war he labored awhile at Fulton, N. Y., and from thence, in 1869, removed to California, and served as pastor at Petaluma ten years.

Thence, he removed to Los Angelos, and in 1882 sustained a severe spinal injury by being thrown from a carriage. This was followed by years of agonizing experience, until he became helpless and so continued until his release by death. Concerning him, a friend writes: " No soldier, not even Garfield or Grant, ever passed to the life beyond, along a more terrible pathway of suffering than he travelled. Yet, as in health, so in sickness, his faith in God was unfaltering. ' He endured, as seeing Him who is invisible.' "

REV. THOMAS STREET, D. D., of Philadelphia was next called this church, and was installed by the Presbytery of Harrisburg, in January, 1860.

He continued in this relation until May, 1864, when he resigned for the purpose of accepting a call to the North Presbyterian Church, New York city, as successor of REV. DR. HATFIELD.

After several prosperous years there, he accepted, partly on reasons of health, a call to the Presbyterian church at Cortland, N. Y. Here he was blessed with many encouraging results, until his ministry was suddenly closed by death. On his way with others, to a meeting of Synod, Oct. 16, 1878, when in the cars conversing with a companion, he was stricken by heart failure, and in a few minutes expired. The period of DR. STREET'S ministry here was one of great divisions, excitements, and controversies throughout the land. When a war so terrible was in progress, a man of prompt, outspoken, loyal impulse, like DR. STREET, could by no means remain silent and undecided. He knew where his convictions and his desires were directed, and it was no doubtful utterance which he made, in the name of God, for Right and Liberty and Union.

After many months of uncertainty and increasing anxiety in regard to another pastor, at length the attention of this church was turned to REV. HENRY E. NILES, of Albion, N. Y. With approval of the Presbyteries having jurisdiction in the case, he accepted a call which was unanimously extended to him, and on the last Sabbath in February, 1865, commenced his ministerial work here.

CHURCH CALENDAR.

SANCTUARY SERVICES—Sunday 10:30 a. m., and 730 p. m.

SUNDAY SCHOOL—From June to October, 9 a. m.; from October to June, 1:30 p. m.

YOUNG PEOPLE'S SOCIETY CHRISTIAN ENDEAVOR—One hour before Sunday evening service.

WEEKLY LECTURE—Wednesday evening, 7:30 or 8 o'clock.

MONTHLY CONCERT FOR MISSIONS—The first Wednesday evening in each month.

SACRAMENT OF THE LORD'S SUPPER—First Sabbath · morning in December, March and June, and second Sabbath in September.

PREPARATORY LECTURE—Friday evening before the Lord's Supper.

LADIES' FOREIGN MISSIONARY SOCIETY—First Wednesday evening in each month.

LADIES' HOME MISSIONARY SOCIETY—Second Wednesday evening.

NILES MISSION BAND—(Young people) Semi-monthly, Friday evening.

WESTMINSTER HOME MISSION BAND—(Young People) Semi-monthly, Friday evening.

ALWAYS READY MISSION BAND—(Juvenile) Semi-monthly.

ANNUAL MEETING OF THE CONGREGATION. The first Wednesday evening in April.

MEMBERSHIP OF THE CHURCH.

THE only condition required of those entering the Communion of the Church, is a credible profession of faith in the Lord Jesus Christ as the personal and only Saviour, and a desire to live in His service, taking the Holy Scriptures as one's rule of life; or a certificate of membership and dismissal from some other Evangelical church.

It is sometimes supposed by those not duly informed on the subject, that each individual member is expected to subscribe to the whole Form of Government, the Westminster Confession and other standards of the Presbyterian denomination. Such pledge is required only of ministers and other officers who are appointed to teach and exercise authority in the Church. But in all cases the standards of the Church are held subordinate to the Holy Scriptures, which are for Christians, the Supreme Rule of Faith and Practice.

ADMISSION OF MEMBERS.

The Session meets regularly after the Preparatory Service to confer with candidates who wish to unite with the Church, either by profession or by letter. At the close of any other service, however, or elsewhere whenever desired, the pastor will be pleased to meet such candidates, and to make arrangements for their introduction.

The baptism of children may, in like manner, be provided for by conference with the pastor.

OFFICERS, 1890.

PASTOR.
HENRY E. NILES, D. D.

ELDERS.
JOHN M. BROWN,   JOSEPH ROOT,
HENRY SMALL,   WM. H. McCLELLAN.

DEACONS.
WM. H. McCLELLAN,   NILES II. SHEARER,
ISAAC A. ELLOITT.

TRUSTEES.
JOHN H. SMALL,   HENRY SMALL,
WM. II. McCLELLAN,   WM. H. GRIFFITH,
GEORGE S. BILLMEYER,   JAMES McLEAN,
E. P. STAIR,   JAS. M. MILLIGAN,
Treasurer.   Secretary.

SEXTON.
WM. P. ZINN.

SYSTEMATIC BENEFICENCE.

Annual offerings are made for the following objects, according to schedules issued at the beginning of each year, for the use of the congregation.

Foreign Missions, ...	January.
Aid for Colleges and Academies.	. February.
Sustentation, . . .	March.
Temperance, ...	April.
Publication (Sunday-school work),	. May.
Home Missions,	. . June.
Church Erection, ...	. July.
Ministerial Relief, .	. September.
Education, .	October.
Home Missions, . . .	. November.
Freedmen (Lincoln University), .	. December.

On each Communion Sabbath an offering for the Deacons' and Sessional Fund.

At each service not specially designated, a collection is taken for the expenses of the church.

ORGANIZATIONS—1890.

WOMAN'S FOREIGN MISSIONARY SOCIETY.

MRS. D. E. SMALL, . . . President.
MRS. H. E. NILES, . . Vice President.
MISS M. B. EVANS, . . . Secretary.
MRS. GEO. S. BILLMEYER, Treasurer.

WOMAN'S HOME MISSIONARY SOCIETY.

MRS. EDWARD CHAPIN, . . . President.
MRS. JOHN H. SMALL, . . . Vice President.
MRS. H. D. RUPP, . Secretary.
MRS. H. A. EBERT, . . . Treasurer.

NILES MISSION BAND (YOUNG PEOPLE).

MRS. H. E. NILES, ... President.
MRS. H. D. RUPP, . . . 1st Vice President.
MISS EMMA L. FISHER, . . 2nd " "
MISS LOUISA L. WALLACE, . 3rd " "
MISS BESSIE PRINCE, . . Secretary.
MISS ANNIE S. WEISER, . . Treasurer.

ALWAYS READY MISSION BAND (JUVENILE).

MISS M. K. KOONS and MISS ANNIE V. RUPP, Managers.

WESTMINSTER MISSION BAND (YOUNG PEOPLE).

MRS. JOHN H. SMALL,   .   .   . President.

Vice President.

Secretary.

Treasurer.

SUNDAY-SCHOOL TEMPERANCE SOCIETY.

HENRY SMALL, ... President.

YOUNG PEOPLE'S SOCIETY OF CHRISTIAN ENDEAVOR.

JOHN HAMILTON SMALL.   . President.

HENRY R. KRABER,   Vice President.

MISS LUCY A. CASE,   .   Secretary.

MISS MINNIE M. GOHN,   Treasurer.

LADIES' AID SOCIETY.

MRS. D. E. SMALL,   .   President.

MRS. WM. A. COOK,   1st Vice President.

MRS. GEO. S. BILLMEYER,   . 2nd "   "

MRS. E. P. STAIR,   ..   . 3rd "   "

MRS. J. A. JONES,   .   .   Secretary.

MRS. W. H. McCLELLAN,   .   Treasurer.

SUNDAY-SCHOOL—1890.

OFFICERS.

JOHN M. BROWN,	Superintendent.
MRS. D. E. SMALL,	Assistant Superintendent.
GEORGE S. BILLMEYER,	Secretary.
J. BAILEY SAYRES,	Treasurer.
MISS JULIA A. SMALL,	Organist.
S. B. HERR,	Chorister.

PRIMARY DEPARTMENT.

MRS. H. W. McCALL,	Superintendent.
MISS FANNIE EVANS,	Assistant Superintendent.
P. A. S. BLAIR,	Organist.

TEACHERS.

JOSEPH ROOT,	MRS. GEORGE S. BILLMEYER,
W. H. McCLELLAN,	MISS MARY KELL,
DR. N. H. SHEARER,	" EMMA L. FISHER,
WM. A. COOK,	" LUCY A. CASE,
HENRY SMALL,	" MARY E. PRINCE,
HENRY C. NILES,	" ANNIE V. RUPP,
CHARLES I. NESS,	" ANNIE STRICKLER,
JAMES M. MILLIGAN,	" JULIA A. SMALL,

JAMES A. KELL,	" KATIE EICHELBERGER,
JOHN H. SMALL,	" M. B. EVANS,
DAVID E. SMALL,	" E. CATHERINE ADAMS,
WM. F. RAMSAY,	" CARRIE B. PATTERSON,
JAMES WEBSTER,	" C. A. WALLACE,
CLAUDE C. CRAVER,	" J. M. QUIGLEY,
MRS. H. E. NILES,	" LOUISA L. WALLACE,
" D. E. SMALL,	" M. R. KOONS,
" EDWARD CHAPIN,	" JULIA DEMUTH,
" W. A. COOK,	" LOUISE WEISER.

PERSONS TEACHING AS SUBSTITUTES.

MRS. JOHN H. SMALL,	MRS. H. D. RUPP,
" W. F. RAMSAY,	" JAMES MCLEAN,
" H. M. CRIDER,	MISS EMMA C. JONES,
W. CARLYLE SMITH,	" ANNA S. WEISER,

DR. J. FRANK SMALL.